P9-CQP-539

J 595.7 O73b
Orme, David, 1948 Mar. 1-
Bugs and spiders /

Bugs and Spiders

by David Orme

Perfection Learning®

Bugs and Spiders

by David Orme

Educational consultant: Helen Bird

Illustrated by Jorge Mongiovi

'Get the Facts' section - images copyright: stick insect Phobaeticus serratipes - Drägü; elephant - Kok Jynn Tan; insects - Robertas P??as; American roach - Marcus Jones; millipede - Paul Marek; flea - Oliver Sun Kim; dust mite - U.S. Food and Drug Administration; louse - Centers for Disease Control and Prevention, U.S. Department of Health and Human Services; 3D rendered mite - Sebastian Kaulitzki; army ants - Mehmet Karatay; Tsetse fly - Geoffrey Attardo; mosquito - U.S. Department of Agriculture; Japanese hornet - Gary Alpert; honey bee - John Severns; locust - Michael Palis; dragonfly fossil - Amanda Rohde; ladybird - Tomasz Pietryszek; maggots - Dalius Baranauskas; Giant African millipede - Denis Ananiadis.

Every effort has been made to locate all copyright holders of material used in this book. If any errors or omissions have occurred, corrections will be made in future editions of this book.

First published in 2009
Copyright © 2009 Ransom Publishing Ltd.
Illustrations copyright © 2009 Jorge Mongiovi
This edition is published by arrangement with Ransom Publishing Ltd.
First American edition 2010

All rights reserved. No part of this book may be used or reproduced, stored in a retrieval system, or transmitted by any means, electronic, mechanical, photocopying, recording, or otherwise, without written permission from the publisher.

Printed in the United States of America

Perfection Learning® Corporation
1000 North Second Avenue
P.O. Box 500
Logan, Iowa 51546-0500
Tel: 1-800-831-4190 • Fax: 1-800-543-2745
perfectionlearning.com

1 2 3 4 5 6 PP 14 13 12 11 10 09
PP/Logan, Iowa, USA
PPI / 10 / 09 , 26870

RLB ISBN-13: 978-1-60686-465-4
RLB ISBN-10: 1-60686-465-3

PB ISBN-13: 978-0-7891-7990-6
PB ISBN-10: 0-7891-7990-3

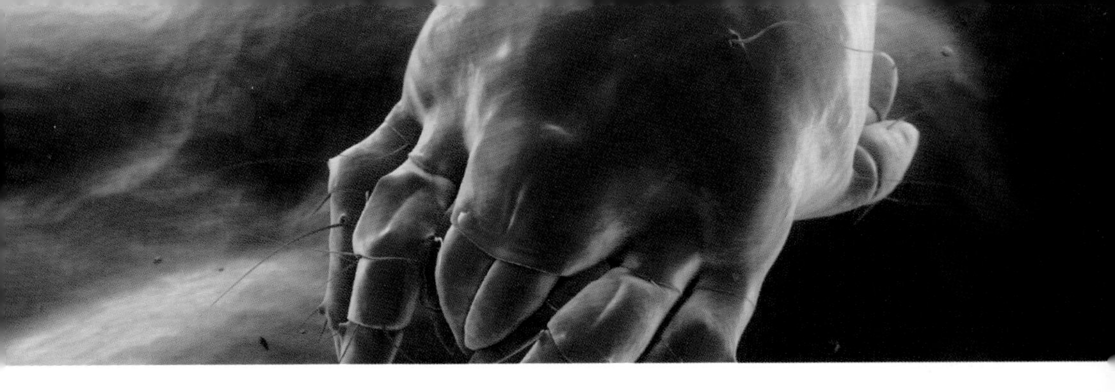

Table of Contents

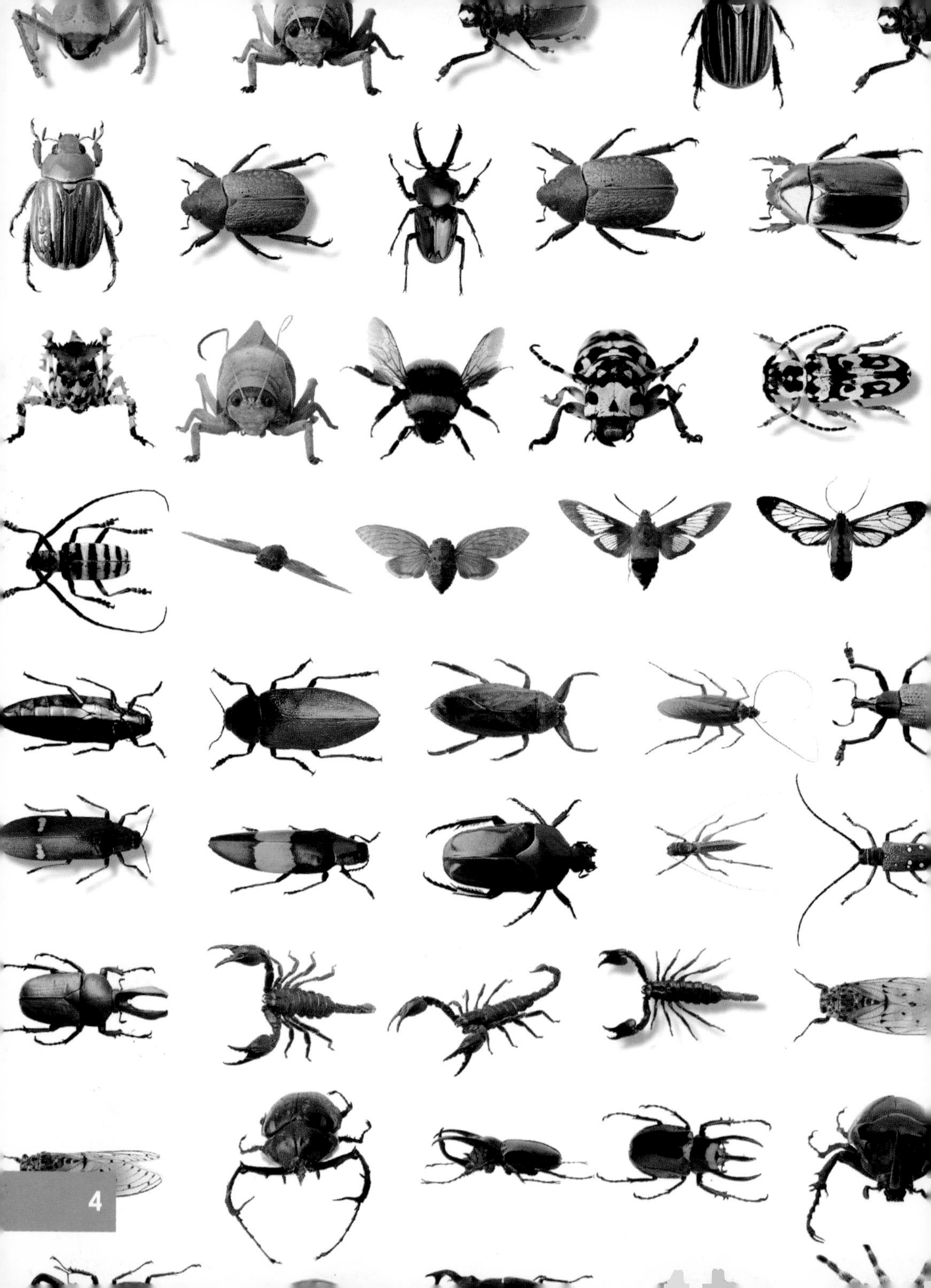

Get the facts

Why are bugs amazing?

Scientists have found:

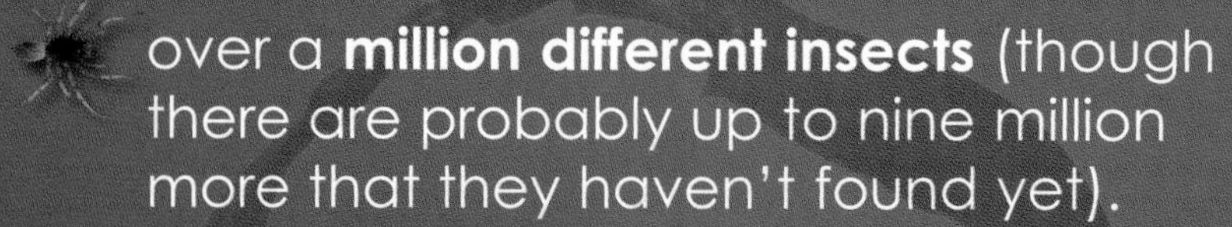

- over a **million different insects** (though there are probably up to nine million more that they haven't found yet).
- over **40,000 different types of spider** (though that's probably less than a quarter of the ones that exist).

They are the **most successful** of all the types of creatures living on the Earth.

How come?

- They can live in many places (**habitats**).
- They live short lives.
- They breed quickly.

This means that they can produce **huge numbers** of themselves.

Fruit fly
Can lay up to 800 eggs every day.
Ready to start breeding after two weeks.

Elephant
Usually has one calf every five years.
Ready to start breeding after 10–12 years.

Bug records

Biggest
Giant Walking Stick Insect. Up to 21 inches long!

Smallest
Fairy fly. Less than 0.008 of an inch long!

Fastest runner
Cockroach —3 mph!

Heaviest
Goliath beetle —about 4 ounces!

Fastest flier
Tabanid fly—90 mph!

Most legs
Insects have 6 legs. But some **millipedes** have around 750 legs.

Spiders

Spider silk is amazing stuff. It is stronger than steel but amazingly light.

250 miles of spider silk would weigh less than 0.2 ounces!

Spiders are smart. They can make different sorts of silk for different jobs:

Extra-strong silk to hold webs in place.

Stickier silk for catching and wrapping up insects.

Very light silk to act like a parachute.

The Weird Fact Box:

In 1973 two spiders called Anita and Arabella were taken into space to see if they could spin webs in zero gravity.

Could they?

Yes—*after a bit of practice.*

Killer spiders

Only around 250 types of spiders are dangerous to people.

These are the two most poisonous spiders:

Funnel Web spider

Brazilian Wandering spider

How deadly?

The **Funnel Web spider** is found in **Australia**. People who are bitten are given antivenom. Even without the antivenom, less than 10% of people who are bitten actually die.

The **Brazilian Wandering spider** is found in **Central** and **South America**. Some types hide in houses. They may bite if they are disturbed. Their venom is the **most deadly** of any spider.

So will their bite kill you?

Not usually. But it hurts a lot!

Human bugs—the yuk! page

Small creatures need places that are warm, safe, and have plenty of stuff to eat. A great place is the **human body**.

People think that because we are **much cleaner** now, we don't have bugs crawling over us.

Don't be so sure.

The flea

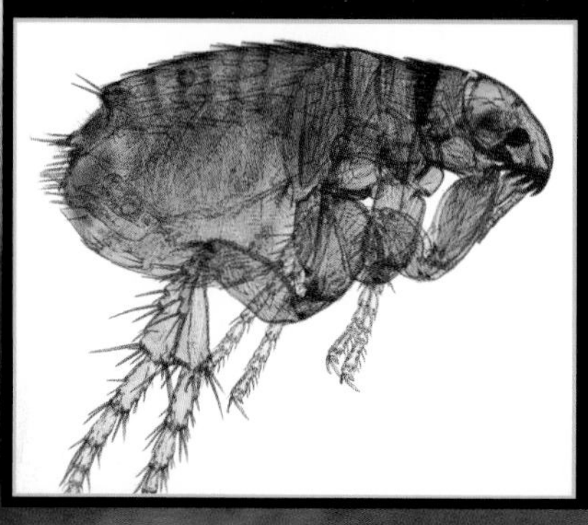

Human fleas aren't found on many people now. But they also live on **pigs**.

So if you shake hands with a friendly pig—watch out!

Body lice

Body lice lurk in your clothes. Then, when you are not expecting it—they start to **suck your blood**. They love blood so much that their bodies **swell up** until they **almost burst**!

Washing clothes—and us—means body

But don't relax. What's that creeping around your head? It's . . .

Head lice

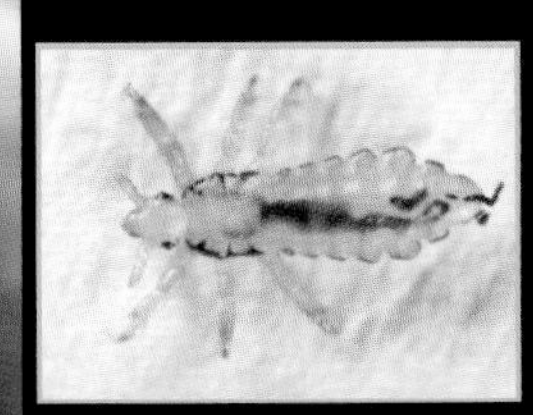

It doesn't matter whether your hair is dirty or clean—head lice just love to be there, **drinking blood** from your scalp!

They inject spit into you to stop the blood clotting. Then they tuck in to a **delicious meal**!

Bed mites

Don't know them? Well, they know you! There are probably around three million of them lurking in your mattress.

They just love the **little flakes of skin** that fall off you all the time—delicious!

Most dangerous

This is the **Giant Japanese hornet**—it is three inches long.

It kills about 70 people a year. Its sting is like "a **red-hot nail** being driven into you."

But the Japanese get revenge—they eat the hornets!

These are **African Army ants** on the march. They can kill and eat animals as big as pigs or goats—so don't hang around!

But these two are not the most deadly.

The **deadliest bugs** are those that spread disease.

This **tsetse fly** causes **sleeping sickness** in people and other diseases in animals. Unless it is treated right away, sleeping sickness is **fatal**.

The **flea** can spread **bubonic plague** to humans. In the past, plagues wiped out at least a third of the population of the world.

So what's the deadliest bug of all?

This one. Mosquitoes spread a disease called **malaria**. It kills around 2 to 3 **million people** every year.

It is definitely the world's most dangerous bug.

Useful bugs

If it wasn't for bugs the world would be full of . . . bugs.

WHY? **Because bugs eat bugs!**

The bugs people really hate are the ones that damage crops by eating them.

The **friendly bugs** are the ones that eat the plant-eating bugs, like this **ladybug**.
These are called **predators**.

People spray **chemicals** that kill the bugs that eat crops.

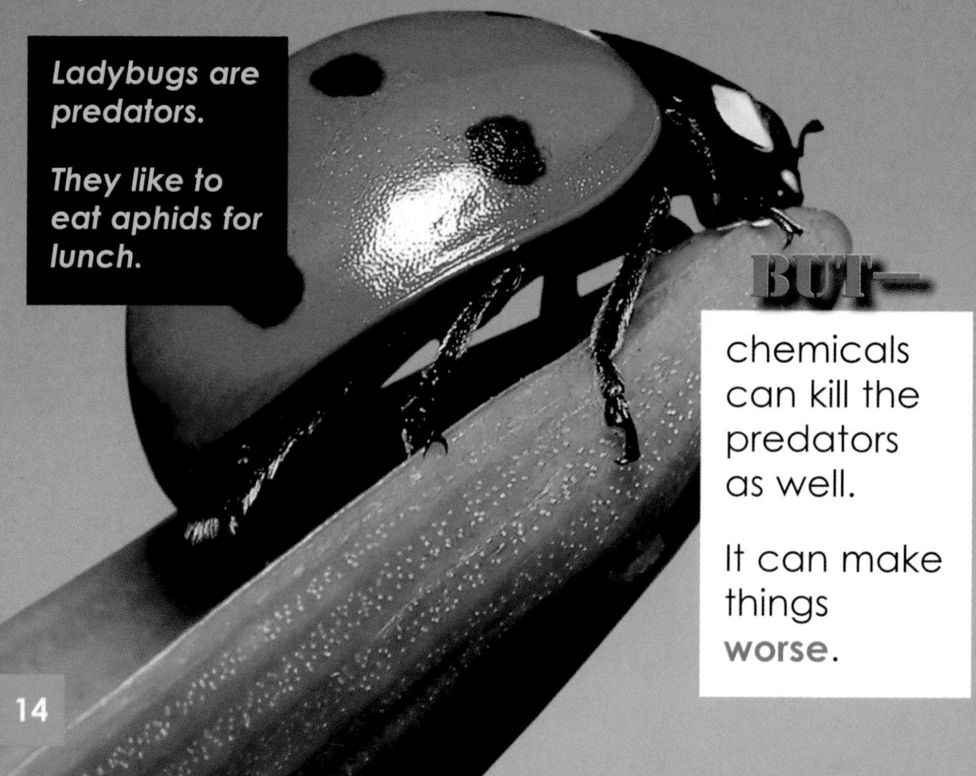

Ladybugs are predators.

They like to eat aphids for lunch.

BUT—

chemicals can kill the predators as well.

It can make things **worse**.

Some insects such as **bees** are important because they spread **pollen** from one plant to another.

Some of these are in danger of disappearing.

WHY?

The **chemicals** can kill them too. And **climate change** may make life difficult for them.

Tasty!

Here's another great use for bugs

—**eat them**!

Bugs make really **healthy food**, and if you cook them well, they're really crunchy!

Mealworms—Stir-fry them and serve with rice. Yummy!

Grasshopper chocolates—Bite into them for a big surprise!

Banana and maggot bread—First, wash and clean the maggots . . .

Giant bugs

Why are bugs small? Why aren't there any **giant bugs**?

It's all about the way they breathe.

Mammals have lungs for breathing. Bugs breathe through **small holes** all over their bodies. These holes lead to small tubes that do the job of lungs.

The trouble is, giant bugs would need really huge breathing tubes, and there wouldn't be room in their bodies.

The Goliath beetle is as big as a bug can get.

I'm just having a breather.

Ancient bugs

Weren't there giant bugs around **millions of years ago**?

YES!

Dragonfly fossils that are as big as large birds have been found.

Millipedes could be as long as a person.

In 2007 the **fossil claw** of a **giant sea scorpion** was found in Germany.

The animal it came from would have been more than **8 feet long**!

But I thought that bugs can't grow that big.

They can't. But millions of years ago, there was **more oxygen** in the air than there is now.

Bugs' breathing tubes could **work better**.

So, maybe on an **alien planet** somewhere, where there is more oxygen in the air . . .

What's
Bugging
You?

Chapter 1
On an alien planet, somewhere . . .

"There's certainly plenty of life on this planet!"

The space exploration team looked at the planet. It was a mass of green and blue.

"Any sign of intelligent life?"

"No radio or TV broadcasts. And I haven't spotted any cities."

The ship went lower.

"This planet is very high in oxygen. We'd better wear helmets."

Just then, the navigator spotted something.

The exploration team has found a new planet . . .
There's certainly plenty of life on this planet!
This planet is very high in oxygen. We'd better wear helmets.

"Hey, check this out! What's that?"

Something that looked like a small, round hill was poking up through the jungle trees.

"That doesn't look natural," said the chief scientist. "Maybe there *is* life on this planet after all."

"There's another one. And another! Those hills are everywhere! There's something going on here!"

"Looks interesting," said the captain. "Let's explore."

Check this out! What's that?
That hill doesn't look natural! Maybe there is life on this planet!
The hills were all over the planet . . .

Chapter 2
Not friendly!

The navigator found a clearing in the forest near one of the strange hills.

The chief scientist got ready to go out. He took the ship's cook with him to act as a guard. They both wore helmets. Too much oxygen would make them feel strange!

They walked toward the hill.

"Hey, there's an opening!" said the cook. "Is it a cave?"

"The walls look too smooth to be a cave. I don't think that's natural."

The chief scientist started exploring the planet.
The ship's cook came as a guard.
There's an opening!
It's not a cave. I wonder what made it?

Things started to happen. Quickly.

A brown head with two huge eyes stared at them from the opening. Then the rest of the creature was out and rushing at them.

"It's an ant! But it's bigger than a person!"

The scientist and the cook turned to run back to the spaceship. Hundreds of the giant ants were pouring out of the opening. And they didn't look friendly.

It’s an ant!
But it’s bigger than
a person!

Chapter 3
The cook gets caught

The scientist reached the airlock just in time. But the cook had eaten too much of his own food. He was slow.

The crew watched helplessly from the airlock as one of the ants picked him up. They were sure that the ants would tear him to pieces.

Then something strange happened.

They ran back to the ship, but
the cook didn't make it . . .
They'll
tear him to
pieces!

All the ants stopped at the same moment. For a second or two, they stood totally still. Then the ant that was holding the cook dropped him to the ground. The huge creatures turned round and started to scuttle back to their giant ant hill.

The captain jumped up and rushed over to the cook.

"Are you all right?"

But the cook didn't speak. Ignoring the captain, he got up and started rushing after the ants!

They're running away! What's going on?
Are you all right?
But the cook wanted to follow the ants . . .

Chapter 4
Being an ant

The captain grabbed the cook and hung on.

"What are you doing?"

But the cook didn't reply. He struggled to get away. Then the crew started yelling. The giant ants had turned back and were rushing toward them!

The braver members of the crew rushed to help. They dragged the cook into the airlock just in time. The ants couldn't break into the tough craft. Within seconds, it was heading for space.

What are you doing?

"So what's it like being an ant?" asked the chief scientist.

"It was weird! I wasn't me anymore. I was one of them!"

"The minds of those ants were linked. That's why they do everything at the same time. Your brain picked up the signals."

"So why did it happen to me and not you?"

"You must have a very special brain, like an ant." said the scientist.

The cook was pleased.

"What's special about an ant's brain, then?"

"It's a very small one!"

I really thought I was an ant!
Your brain picked up the signals the ants were sending to each other. You must have a special brain, like an ant!
How is my brain like an ant's?
It's a very small one!

Bugs and Spiders word check

anti-venom
bubonic plague
chemicals
climate change
clotting
deadly
fatal
habitat
malaria
millipede
mosquito
oxygen
parachute
poisonous
pollen
predator
sleeping sickness
tsetse fly
venom
zero gravity